Sources of Historical Banking Panics: A Markov Switching Approach

Abstract

Around the turn of the previous century banking panics in the U.S. happened fairly

frequently. Before the creation of the Federal Reserve, major financial crises occurred in

the United States in 1873, 1884, 1890, 1893, and 1907. Using a Markov-switching

model (MSM) and weekly data between 1890 and 1909, we examine periods of panic and

periods of relative calm and objectively date the onset and conclusion of the banking

panics. The MSM also has imbedded within it a mechanism that allows us to examine

the economic circumstances that might have precipitated a banking panic. This feature

allows us to compare empirically several different hypotheses about what triggers a

banking panic.

The underlying causes of banking panics are still very much up for debate. Widespread banking panics or even runs on a single bank are a rarity in the modern financial environment of the United States. The extent to which the modern financial environment (with regulation, deposit insurance, and a flexible money supply) is the cause of this stability, the aspects that are required for stability, and the question of whether the additional costs and agency problems are worth the additional stability are still hotly contested by academics and regulators. The primary goal of this paper is to examine the triggers of banking panics and compare competing hypotheses about the underlying causes of banking panics in the National Banking Era (1863–1913).

Although banking panics are now rare in the United States, they were considerably more common around the turn of the previous century. During the National Banking era (before the creation of the Federal Reserve System), major banking panics occurred in the United States in 1873, 1884, 1890, 1893, and 1907.

There is an ongoing controversy in the literature about the causes of these banking panics. The participants generally fall into two camps: those who see these panics as essentially a problem of illiquidity and those who base their explanations on insolvency.

The earliest papers that looked at these crises were written by those who were alive at the time of the panics, and were largely descriptive in nature. Most contemporaries of the banking panics saw these panics as liquidity-driven events associated with an unusual spike in domestic demand for cash or international demand for gold. These changes in the demand for money were met with a "perverse elasticity," as money left the banking system and there was essentially no ability to change the monetary base. These theories of banking panics as largely based on illiquidity led to the foundation of the Federal Reserve System.

A more recent set of papers and models view banking panics fundamentally as a function of bank insolvency. These papers argue that changes in the business cycle (or some other signal of a change in expected return) induced depositors to update their expectations of the banks' abilities to repay them, and these revised expectations led depositors to withdraw their funds from all banks because of asymmetric information about which particular banks were holding questionable assets.

Each theoretical approach has found backing in econometric studies. Empirical papers have generally used the dates of panics from studies produced for the National Monetary Commission—such studies, for example, as Sprague (1910) and Kemmerer (1910). However, these authors, and thus the subsequent authors that refer to them, differ on the events that constituted banking panics and on the dates that represent the beginnings and ends of the panics. These differences in what is considered a panic and in the relevant dates may partly explain the differences in conclusions. In addition, the econometric papers often use data that are in monthly or quarterly frequencies, and such data would be likely to emphasize the differences in the behavior of variables during panics rather than catching what is associated with the onset of a panic—that is, the trigger.

To overcome these problems of dating panics and observing the triggers of panics, we are proposing a new approach to both dating the panics and examining the variables that are associated with going into (and out of) a banking panic. The Markov Switching Model uses the data themselves to determine the starting and ending points of banking panics. The Markov Switching Model also has the advantage that it is possible to parameterize the probability of transitioning into (and out of) a banking panic and to see what variables have actually been associated with triggering banking panics.

We use the Markov Switching Model method and weekly interest-rate data from the callable loan market to identify panic periods. The dates we find for panics are consistent with, but not exactly the same as, those from the more subjective dating methods used by other authors. The high frequency of our data allows us a great deal of precision in our dates for panic periods. In addition, we are able to use the estimation of the probabilities of transitioning into and out of a panic period to test a variety of potential triggers for banking panics. We derive the list of potential triggers from both sides of the illiquidity vs. insolvency debate mentioned above. We find the greatest amount of support for the traditional view of banking panics as driven by liquidity issues.

Literature

There are a number of theoretical models of what might cause a financial panic. With banks holding a fractional reserve, a loss of confidence in the banks' ability to repay deposits can cause a run on deposits. A number of theoretical models have been put forward suggesting what might cause such a loss in confidence.

As noted above, the basic views fall into two camps: an illiquidity-driven panic vs. an insolvency-driven panic. The first group focuses on the nature of banks with long-term assets and short-term liabilities, à la Diamond and Dybvig (1983). This perspective on banks is that banks are held together by the common self-fulfilling expectation that deposits will be repaid. If something changes the expectations of repayment, then depositors run the fractional reserve bank or banking system, which is also a self-fulfilling equilibrium (see also Chari and Jagannathan, 1988). Other work, such as Bhattacharya and Gale (1987), has focused on what kinds of triggers or signals might cause expectations to change and thus cause a run on a bank.

Kemmerer (1910), who was contemporaneous with the National Banking Era, notes that crises were more likely to occur during periods when the liquidity of the fractional reserve system was already under strain, usually during the planting and harvesting seasons, when non-money-center banks withdrew their deposits. Miron (1986) documents the view that crises were much more common in the autumn, when demands for currency were high because of agricultural activity. Interest rates and reserve ratios also showed a clear pattern associated with the agricultural seasons. Eichengreen (1984) formalizes this observation with a model of checking and currency deposits, with the feature that money flowed to low-check-use areas of the country during the periods of the year when demand for money was highest in order to move crops. Thus the money supply fell when the demand for money was highest, exhibiting a "perverse elasticity."

During the National Banking Era (1863–1913), although banking panics were common in the United States, Canada and Great Britain did not have systemwide bank panics. By comparing the experience of the Canadian and U.S. banking systems in the late nineteenth and early twentieth centuries, both Williamson (1989) and Bordo, Redish, and Rockoff (1996) suggest that the branch banking system of Canada was more diversified and better able to weather adverse economic shocks. In the same vein, Chari (1989) extends the Diamond and Dybvig (1983) model to include community risk, where the proportion of impatient people varies by community. For a banking system without branching, the community risk is also the banks' risk, and overcoming this risk requires interbank lending and verifiable reserves. However, Champ, Smith, and Williamson (1996) point out that in contrast to the U.S. system, where large withdrawals of gold and other base money were required to satisfy an increased currency demand during harvest seasons, Canadian banks also had more flexibility to issue additional banknotes when currency demand was high, and thus were not forced to contract in order to satisfy an increased demand for currency.

Jevons (1884) blames banking panics on unexpected events in conjunction with seasonal liquidity problems, which combine to undermine the depositors' confidence in the system and leads to runs and the cascade of events. Sprague (1910), Freidman and Schwartz (1963), and Tallman and Moen (1998) emphasize an international component to banking panics, including gold outflows or increases in the Bank of England discount rate. Inability to offset the fall in bank reserves by increasing the money supply exacerbated the contractions and set off crises. Sprague (1910) and Dewald (1972) focus on the response of the New York money-center banks when faced with unusually high demands for cash given their inflexible and conservative reserve ratios of 25 percent minimum set by the clearinghouse association. They hold that it was this inflexibility that led to the crises.

The strand of literature that focuses on insolvency as leading to panics generally concentrates on when in the business cycle the panics occur (Gorton, 1988; Calomiris and Gorton, 1991; Kindleberger, 1978). These authors note that crises tend to occur near the peak of a business cycle, and suggest that changes in the expected profitability of firms lead to either a contraction in lending or a banking/financial crisis or both. In the model by Calomiris and Gorton (1991), the source of panics is based on information asymmetry in the bank-depositor relationship. As the economy heads into recession, depositors notice that business profits are declining and may expect banks that lent heavily to troubled businesses to fail. To avoid potential losses, depositors withdraw their funds if they expect their bank to fail. However, depositors cannot easily observe the true liquidation value of bank assets because bank loans are not traded in secondary markets. With asset values uncertain, depositors cannot differentiate good banks from bad banks; as a result, depositors then run all banks since they are uncertain about the likelihood that their own bank(s) will fail. The bank panic forces a suspension of convertibility so that the solvency of individual banks can be assessed. The clearinghouse has a pivotal role in establishing the credibility of the workout of insolvent banks. According to these models, the likelihood of a panic should increase as the macroeconomy is moving into a recession.

A common feature of empirical papers on banking panics in this period is that they use information on panics derived from papers produced for the National Monetary Commission or another subjective dating system.[1] Sprague (1910) mentions panics that occurred in 1873, 1884, 1890, 1893, and 1907. Kemmerer (1910) finds 21 minor panics or "panicky periods" between 1876 and 1908.[2] The subjective system of enumerating these panics leads to discrepancies about whether something actually constitutes a crisis and about the dating for the onsets and conclusions of these panics. It may be that some of the variation in the results found by the empirical studies can be traced back to the underlying uncertainty about the panics themselves.

In a study that represents a springboard for our investigation, Donaldson (1992) performs an empirical investigation of these historical panics and finds that "panics are 'special events,' in the sense that panic and non-panic data are generated by different economic systems."[3] If the data were indeed generated by different economic systems, one way to examine these historical crises would be by using a Markov Switching Model. A switching model assumes a data-generating process that changes across time, and such a model would allow for differences in the process by which interest rates were determined during panic and non-panic periods. By differentiating between these data-generating processes, we have an objective marker for the beginning of the panic and its

---

[1] The empirical papers include Canova (1994), Donaldson (1992), Miron (1986), and Calomiris and Gorton (1991).
[2] These were documented in what Kemmerer (p. 223) describes as "a rather hasty perusal of the Chronicle for the years 1876 to 1908."
[3] Donaldson (1992), 277–78.

end. This objective marker will improve our ability to distinguish the true triggers of episodes of panic.

We use a switching model to examine short-term interest rates in this historical period. Regime-switching models have been used to examine interest rates in the modern era. Much of the work on interest rates being driven by changes in parameters over time is based on Hamilton (1989), who models discrete shifts in the underlying parameters driving short-term interest rates. Gray (1996) develops a generalized regime-switching model to examine short-term interest rates, which includes Markov switching of states as well as conditional heteroskedasticity component to the variance in the states. Ang and Bekaert (2002) look at the econometric performance of the regime-switching models in general for interest rates in a number of countries.

Background

The banking system in the National Banking Era was structured with a tiered reserve system. National banks in central reserve cities were required to hold a 25 percent reserve on deposits in gold, coin, or cash in vault.[4] National banks not in reserve cities were required to hold a 15 percent reserve, of which 60 percent could be held as deposits in reserve city or central reserve city banks. Reserve city banks could also hold a proportion of their reserves as deposits in the central reserve city banks. In addition to being reserves for the non-reserve-city banks, these deposits, or bankers' balances, paid interest and facilitated the clearing of transactions. The banks in reserve cities or central reserve cities were commercial banks and not connected to a governmental body. The

---

[4] New York, Chicago, St. Louis, Boston, Baltimore, Cincinnati, New Orleans, Philadelphia, and Providence were listed as redemption cities by the 1863 National Bank Act. The list of redemptions cities was modified by the 1864 revision of the National Bank Act. In 1887 an amendment to the law gave cities of 50,000 or greater the ability to become reserve cities, and cities of 200,000 or more the ability to become central reserve cities. This is when St. Louis and Chicago were added to New York City as central reserve cities.

reserve requirements of the reserve city banks meant that some of what were "reserves" from the non-reserve city (sometimes referred to as "country") banks could be loaned out in turn by the reserve city banks.[5]

Banks in the reserve cities organized themselves into clearinghouse associations to facilitate the clearing of interbank transactions. The clearinghouse cleared transactions between banks, but it was also an organization of member banks, where mutual trust was an important part of the clearing process. Thus, clearinghouses had both the ability and the incentive to monitor the activities of member banks and could exact penalties from imprudent banks. In times of crisis the clearinghouse could elect to clear transactions on the basis of clearinghouse loan certificates, which were the mutual obligation of all the clearinghouse members.[6]

Because of its position as the center of international commerce in the United States, New York was the most important of the central reserve cities, and New York City banks held by far the largest proportion of the reserves of correspondent country banks.

Many of the bankers' balances held by the New York clearinghouse banks were loaned to participants in the stock market on the callable loan market.[7] Call loans could be demanded the same day and were basically overnight loans. The call loan interest rate reflected a competitive price on new loans, and the rate of interest for call loans that were renewed, or rolled over, was tied to the average interest rate for new loans that day. The loans were collateralized by the stock that was purchased, and a margin of 20 percent was required. Because of the nature of call loans—they were collateralized with stock, were short term, and were callable on demand—these loans were perceived as a very liquid

---

[5] Moen and Tallman (2003).
[6] Calomiris and Gorton (1991), Cannon (1910).
[7] Moen and Tallman (2003).

and safe investment by New York clearinghouse banks.[8] Banks optimized their portfolios across different types of investments, and the most liquid were considered to be call loans. As Myers (1931) puts it, "Banks invested in commercial paper, which usually bore a higher rate of interest than call loans, all the funds which they dared to tie up for a considerable length of time. Into the call loan market they put only those funds which they were holding against momentary withdrawal."[9] Thus the funds in the call market were there to some extent because they could be liquidated immediately if a bank felt the need. This characteristic gave the call market a very close tie to the reserve position of the banks.

Under normal circumstances call market loans carried a lower interest rate than commercial paper, and banks would optimize their portfolios between the longer- and shorter-term loans on the basis of credit quality and opportunity cost.[10] The generally lower interest rate on call market loans highlights the fact that these loans were considered safer than commercial paper. However, although the call market was a good place to lend money that a bank might need to liquidate quickly for an idiosyncratic risk, it proved to be unstable when there was a broad-based need to liquidate these loans. When a large number of the New York reserve banks were facing a need to liquidate their call loans, such as during a banking panic when several banks would face large withdrawal demands simultaneously, interest rates in the call loan market would become very high and unstable. It is these systemic events in the call market, and the spikes in call market interest rates that went with them, that we are examining as an indicator of a banking panic.

---

[8] Myers (1931).
[9] Ibid., 135.
[10] Ibid.

11

We use the call market interest rate in the Markov Switching Model framework to detect banking panics. The call market interest rate is a competitive interest rate in a market that has many participants on both sides of the transactions and in which liquidity is tightly linked to the reserve positions of the New York banks. In addition, the interest rate is available at very high frequency: weekly. For all these reasons, the call market interest rate is an excellent indicator variable for seeing when depositor withdrawals were widespread and substantial enough to cause serious liquidity problems for banks.

Empirical Approach and Data

The Markov Switching Model is designed to pick out changes in the generating mechanism of a variable. The model assumes more than one type of distribution, or generating mechanism, and an imperfect ability to observe when the switch between generating mechanisms occurs. The pattern in the call loan market interest rates of periods of stability with low interest rates and periods of instability with high interest rates is the type of pattern that might be best explained by shifts in the underlying behavior generating the observed variable. If these shifts in behavior were associated with banking panics, then the empirical observation would align well with the theoretical explanation that the changes in interest rates came from a broad-based withdrawal of liquidity by constrained banks.

The model that we are using in this paper characterizes the interest rates from the call market as coming from two different generating mechanisms or states, which we have labeled as a panic or a non-panic state. The model estimates a probability of being in a panic or non-panic state on the basis of the information inherent in the data, giving us an objective approach to dating the panic periods. Our estimation method allows us to resolve differences in the categorization and the timing of panic periods. Other estimation techniques are often very dependent on the timing of an event, which can be fairly subjective and can sometimes substantially affect the results.

In addition, the Markov Switching Model assumes that shifting between panic and non-panic states is defined by transition probabilities. By estimating the probabilities of transitioning between the two states, we are able to compare differing hypotheses about the sources of these panics empirically. We can observe if a particular variable is associated with an increase in the probability of the start of a panic. For example, one can parameterize this transition probability with measures of macroeconomic activity, and the significance of these variables would support the asymmetric information theory of bank panics. Alternative theories can be tested in an identical manner and can also be compared with one another.

The Data

Panics are sometimes short events lasting in some cases only a few weeks or even days. Therefore, we based our analysis on the highest-frequency data available—weekly observations. The data series that we were able to obtain in a weekly frequency are shown in table 1, with their means and standard deviations. Our data set includes weekly observations from 1890 through 1909 on the call market interest rate, net flows of cash from New York City banks to the interior, excess reserves, discount rate of the Bank of England, the exchange rate of the dollar to the British pound, net gold imports, broad stock index changes, and commercial failures. These data allow us to compare directly a number of possible panic triggers mentioned in the literature.

Table 1:
Summary Statistics

Variable	Variable Name	Obs.	Mean (Std Dev)
Interest Rates			
Call Loan Interest Rate	Callrate	1043	3.65 (3.62)
Difference in Call Loan Interest Rate	difclrt	1042	−0.0005 (2.924)
Liquidity			
Net Movement of Deposits	netmvmt	1043	1.40 (3.93)
Excess Reserves	exres	1043	20.84 (20.11)
International			
Bank of England Discount Rate	BoE_disc	1042	3.30 (1.03)
Change in BoE Discount Rate	ch_disc	1041	0.0014 (0.240)
$/£ Exchange Rate	Exch_lb	986	4.87 (0.02)
Change in $/£	ch_Exch	985	0.0000 (0.006)
Net Gold Flows	goldflow	1043	388,887 (2,818,040)
Business Cycle			
Percent Change in Stock Value	pctchsv	1043	0.077 (2.066)
Commercial Failures	commfail	990	222.3 (63.9)
Change in Commercial Failures	ch_fail	989	0.057 (34.403)

The indicator variable used by the Markov Switching Model to delineate banking panics is the Difference in Call Loan Interest Rate (*difclrt*). The Call Loan Interest Rate averaged 3.65 between 1890 and 1909, with a sizable standard deviation. This pattern of alternating periods of low interest rates and high interest rates can be seen in figure 1 and represents the heart of our use of a regime-switching model. For testing competing hypotheses about the triggers of panics, in some of the cases we used the change in variables rather than the level, that is, Change in Bank of England Discount Rate (*ch_disc*), Change in $/£ Exchange Rate (*ch_Exch*), Percent Change in Stock Value (*pctchsv*), and Change in Commercial Failures (*ch_fail*). We used the variables Net Movement of Deposits (*netmvmt*) and Excess Reserves (*exres*) in levels, expressed in millions of dollars. The data series in table 1 comes from Kemmerer (1910), supplemented by various issues of the Commercial and Financial Chronicle.

The Model

The Markov Switching Model assumes the existence of two (or more) states and assumes, as well, that the state is not perfectly observable. The pattern of observed realizations of the time series variable is driven by switches between the underlying distributions, or states. These switches between the states evolve in first-order Markov process.

In our specific version of the more generalized model, there are two states: a normal state and a panic state. The state variable is $S_t = 0, 1$, where zero indicates a normal state and one indicates a panic. In each period there is a probability that the state will transition into the other state. The transition probability of changing from a normal state into a panic would be $Pr(S_t = 1| S_{t-1} = 0, x_t)$, and the probability of staying in the normal state would be $Pr(S_t = 0| S_{t-1} = 0, x_t) = (1-Pr(S_t = 1| S_{t-1} = 0, x_t))$, where x_t is a set of variables that affect the probability of transitioning between states. If $Pr(S_t = 0| S_{t-1} = 0, x_t)$ rises, the probability of switching into a panic state declines. It is this transition probability that we parameterize in order to test which variables had an effect on the probability of a crisis occurring. Similarly, there is a probability of staying in the panic state, so that we are also able to examine which factors may influence the ending of a crisis.

Figure 2 plots the first differences of weekly observations of the average interest rate charged on call loans at the NYSE for the period 1890–1909. Periods of calm are characterized by relatively stable interest rates, whereas the likely panic periods are characterized by extremely volatile interest rates. The variable that is being acted on by the state variable is the change in the call market interest rate, $\Delta r_t \equiv r_t - r_{t-1}$. The realization of this variable is a function of a state-dependent mean and variance.

$$\Delta r_t \equiv \mu_{it} + \sqrt{h_{it}}\, z_t \tag{1}$$

for $S_t = i$. Here, for a given state, μ_{it} and h_{it} define the conditional mean and conditional variance, respectively, and z_t is an independent and identically distributed random variable with mean zero and unit variance. The conditional mean and conditional variance are specified to capture two well-known empirical attributes of short-term interest rates. First, any model of short-term interest rates must capture the important characteristic that the short rate is mean reverting. The simplest and most common way of modeling mean reversion is to let the change in the short rate depend linearly on the level of last period's short rate. For each state, the functional form of the conditional mean incorporates mean reversion in this way and is specified by

$$\mu_{it} = a_{0i} + a_{1i} r_{t-1}. \tag{2}$$

In addition to mean reversion, the unconditional distribution of changes in the short rate is known to be leptokurtic—that is, "fat tailed." Engle (1982) shows that a possible cause of the leptokurtosis in the unconditional distribution is conditional heteroskedasticity. Two ways of modeling this conditional heteroskedasticity are common in the literature. One can either use the ARCH/GARCH models of Engle (1982) and Bollerslev (1986) or simply specify the conditional variance of changes in the short rate as a function of the level of the short rate. We choose the latter approach and specify the conditional variance process of each regime as

$$h_{it} = \exp(b_{0i} + b_{1i}r_{t-1}) \tag{3}$$

A comparison of figure 1 (the level of call market interest rates) with figure 2 (the change in call market interest rates) provides justification for this specification: as the interest rates increased, the volatility also escalated.

The states are not directly observed, so for every observation there is an estimated probability of being in a given state. The Markov Switching Model also calculates the transition probabilities and the distributions within the two states. The "Results" section below describes the pattern of the estimated probability of being in normal or panic state as it evolves over time and describes the relationship between the possible panic trigger variables and the time-varying transition probabilities. More detail about the process by which the Markov Switching Model estimates these parameters is given in the appendix.

Results

The Markov Switching Model assumes that the data are derived from more than one generating mechanism or distribution. However, although some previous research such as Donaldson (1992) find results that suggest that changes in the generating mechanism, others such as Calomiris and Gorton (1991) find that the major variables moved in a way that was consistent across panic and non-panic periods. Using the test from Garcia (1998), we tested call market interest rates to see if they were more consistent with having been generated by one distribution or with having been generated by two; we rejected the one-state null at above the 99 percent confidence level.

We use the weekly call market data within the Markov Switching Model setting, first to determine the beginning and ending points of panic periods and then to parameterize the transition probabilities to shed light on triggering events. The first step, that of examining the dating of the panic periods, uses constant transition probabilities. We show that the model does a very credible job of identifying financial panics that

17

occurred during the time period under consideration. Once the panics have been identified, their causes will be determined when we reestimate the model by parameterizing the transition probabilities.

Constant Transition Probability Model

The first step was to estimate the model with constant transition probabilities so that we could focus on the process of finding the best structure for the underlying call market interest-rate data and dating panics and the switches in the data into and out of the panic state.

Table 2 is broken into parameters for the normal and panic states. The stub indicates the parameters for the distributions of the normal and panic states. The names of the independent variables are found in column 1, and the remaining columns provide the estimation results for the different regime-switching models. These columns contain the coefficients for the conditional mean and conditional variances of the panic and normal periods and the probability of staying in a given state. In table 2 the probability of switching states is a constant. In the subsection "Time-Varying Transition Probabilities" below, we will examine the effect other variables may have on increasing or decreasing the probability of entering or leaving a panic state.

The models each identify a low and a high interest-rate state. The columns represent different models with regard to the estimation of variance for each of the two states. Column 2 has constant variances within each state. Column 3 has conditional heteroskedasticity in the variance of the (high interest-rate) panic state but not of the (low interest-rate) normal state. Column 4 has conditional heteroskedasticity in the normal state but not in the panic state. And the rightmost column calculates a model with conditional heteroskedasticity in both states. When the log likelihood ratio test is used, the rightmost column with the conditional heteroskedasticity for both variances has the best fit.

Most of the observations fell into the normal, or non-panic, state, which had a low interest rate, averaging 2.9 percent, and a low variance. The negative sign on *Callrate_lag*, the level of last period's short rate, confirms that interest rates in this state are mean reverting. In other words, interest rates in this regime will tend to revert to the low rate of 2.9 percent. For the panic periods the average interest rate is 9.2 percent, and again the negative sign of the coefficient indicates that in the panic state as well, the interest rates tend to be mean reverting.

We estimated volatility by specifying the variance as an exponential function. That is, we rewrote equation (5) as $h_{it} = \exp(b_{0i} + b_{1i}r_{t-1})$. For both the panic and normal states, the coefficient for the interest rate, *CallRate_lag*, is positive; therefore, in both the panic and normal states the variance increases with interest rate. For the normal state, if the interest rate were near its average of 2.9 percent, the variance would be about 0.16 percentage points. In the panic state, again if the interest rate were near its average of 9.2 percent, the variance would be 44.5 percentage points.

We estimated the transition probability parameters by specifying the transition probabilities as a standard normal distribution function. The probability of staying in the normal (non-panic) state, $\Pr(S_t = 0 \mid S_{t-1} = 0)$, in the next period is 1.56 on the standard normal distribution, or a 94.1 percent probability in the full conditional heteroskedasticity model in the rightmost column. Thus, the probability of shifting into a financial crisis is about 6 percent, and this probability does not change across the entire sample period for these models. Similarly, the probability of shifting out of a financial panic is about 44 percent, and this probability is also constant across the entire sample period.

Table 2:
Constant Transition Probabilities

	Independent Variables	No Conditional Heteroskedasticity	Conditional Heteroskedasticity in Panic Periods	Conditional Heteroskedasticity in Normal Periods	Conditional Heteroskedasticity in Both
Normal					
Conditional Mean	Constant	0.173 ***	0.151 ***	0.091 ***	0.096 ***
		(0.035)	(0.033)	(0.026)	(0.026)
	Callrate_lag	-0.084 ***	-0.082 ***	-0.042 ***	-0.047 ***
		(0.014)	(0.013)	(0.014)	(0.014)
Variance	Constant	-1.944 ***	-2.266 ***	-4.124 ***	-4.172 ***
		(0.081)	(0.094)	(0.143)	(0.140)
	Callrate_lag			0.792 ***	0.790 ***
				(0.041)	(0.041)
Transition Probability	p_0	1.488 ***	1.452 ***	1.606 ***	1.562 ***
		(0.080)	(0.088)	(0.084)	(0.085)
	(probability)	93.2%	92.7%	94.6%	94.1%
Panic					
Conditional Mean	Constant	4.054 ***	1.791 **	5.487 ***	4.668 ***
		(0.569)	(0.716)	(0.988)	(1.128)
	Callrate_lag	-0.536 ***	-0.178	-0.565 ***	-0.467 ***
		(0.059)	(0.142)	(0.082)	(0.168)
Variance	Constant	3.334 ***	1.587 ***	3.896 ***	3.140 ***
		(0.105)	(0.337)	(0.150)	(0.292)
	Callrate_lag		0.196 ***		0.071 **
			(0.046)		(0.030)
Transition Probability	Constant	0.688 ***	0.891 ***	0.139	0.154
		(0.122)	(0.125)	(0.171)	(0.169)
	(probability)	75.4%	81.3%	55.5%	56.1%
Value of Objective Function =		-1301.67	-1277.79	-1106.49	-1099.44

Note: Standard errors are in parentheses.
* Indicates significance at the 10% level.
** Indicates significance at the 5% level.
*** Indicates significance at the 1% level.

The model identifies a low interest-rate state and a high interest-rate state. Since these states are not directly observable, the model estimates a probability for each observation of being in the high or low interest-rate state. Specifically, we use the smoothed probabilities to identify the panic periods because these probabilities use all the information across the sample. In our sample period, 1890–1909, we found five substantial panics and three minor panics. Figures 3 through 9 show the probability of panic for each of the years for which we found a panic period. In most cases the probability of being in a panic is near zero except for a few observations in the panic state, where the probability is close to one. We summarize these findings in table 3, where we compare our dates with those of six other sources.

Table 3
Financial Panics 1890–1909

Year	McDill and Sheehan	Kemmerer	Sprague	Canova	Donaldson	Miron	Calomiris and Gorton
1890	Major: Aug. 16	Major: Nov. 10	Major: Nov.10	Major	Major	Major	Major: November
1893	Major: Mar. 4 Jun. 10	Major: May 5 (or Feb 20)	Major: Feb. 26	Major	Major	Major	Major: June-August
1896	Minor: Oct. 31	Minor: December					Minor: October
1899	Minor: Dec. 16	Major: Late December		Major		Major	
1901		Major: May 9		Major		Major	
1903		Major: March		Major		Major	
1905	Major: Nov. 4	Minor: April					
1906	Major: Dec. 8	Minor: December					
1907	Minor: Mar. 16 Major: Oct. 26	Major: March and October	Major: Oct. 21	Major	Major	Major	Major: October

Note: The dates for McDill/Sheehan are the beginning of the week in which the panic occurred. Minor panics from Kemmerer (1910, pp. 222–23) were derived from a list of "panicky periods."

Specifically, besides the present paper, the table refers to three other empirical studies of historical financial panics—Canova (1994), Donaldson (1992), and Miron (1986)—as well as the two sources that those three studies generally used as the basis of their dating for the panics: Kemmerer (1910) and Sprague (1910). In addition we included in table 3 the banking panic dates of Calomiris and Gorton (1991), who set their own criteria for the definition of a banking panic. They defined banking panics as episodes of widespread suspension of convertibility by banks, episodes when clearinghouse loan certificates were issued, and episodes where the clearinghouses perceived a need to forestall suspensions. In each of the empirical studies, the dates of the financial panics are assumed, and analysis of this time period involves dummy variables for the dates of these crises. Notice that Donaldson (1992), based on Sprague (1910), assumes fewer major panics than either Canova (1994) or Miron (1986), both of whom looked to Kemmerer (1910) for panic dates.

In general the Markov Switching Model approach closely matches the panics found by other authors, while allowing the data to speak for themselves about the dating of the crisis periods.

Time-Varying Transition Probabilities

At this point we investigate the possible triggers for moving into (and out of) a panic state. One of the earliest explanations (Kemmerer, 1910), which found favor later in the work of Miron (1986) and Eichengreen (1984), is that of seasonal movements in deposits from the reserve banks to the interior country banks because of seasonal demand for cash needed for planting, harvesting, and moving crops to market. We look at the variable *netmvmt*, which is the net movement of deposits from the country banks to the reserve center banks for the week.

A related possibility is that the depositors were carefully watching the levels of excess reserves, *exres*, and running the banks if the reserves threatened to get so low that banks might have trouble repaying deposits. This possibility is very much within the realm of Chari and Jagannathan (1988), Chari (1989), and Williamson (1989).

We also examine the effect of gold flows in order to examine the possibility that domestic panics were a result of foreign inflows/outflows. In addition, we test changes in the Bank of England discount rate and changes in the exchange rate with the British pound. We include these variables in order to examine the effect of international triggers as suggested by Sprague (1910), Friedman and Schwartz (1963), and Tallman and Moen (1998).

We also investigate the change in the stock market week to week, in case the spikes in call market interest rates are the result of sharp declines in stock market values. If the tightening of the call market interest rate is a function of declines in the values of the collateral, then the falls in the stock market should lead the rises in the call market interest rates. If the direction of causation runs from banks withdrawing liquidity in order to satisfy depositor demands, then the call market interest rates pattern should lead the stock market changes. In addition, stock market values are forward looking about expected business activity, and this quality should give us some ability to examine the expected-recession hypothesis of Gorton (1988) and Calomiris and Gorton (1991). Commercial failures should also give us a sense of the business climate at the time the panics began.

The net movement of deposits appears to have a strong effect on the probability of going into a panic state. The positive sign on the coefficient for *netmvmt* in column 2 of table 4 indicates that the greater the inflow of deposits to the money-center banks, the higher the probability of staying in the non-panic, or normal, state. Conversely, as deposits drain from the money-center banks, the probability of a panic increases.

Table 4:
Liquidity Variables

	Independent Variables	Net Deposit Movement		Excess Reserves		Net Deposit Movement & Ex. Reserves	
Normal							
Conditional Mean	Constant	0.124	***	0.159	***	0.163	***
		(0.024)		(0.025)		(0.025)	
	Callrate_lag	-0.085	***	-0.091	***	-0.093	***
		(0.012)		(0.013)		(0.013)	
Conditional Variance	Constant	-4.159	***	-4.043	***	-4.002	***
		(0.119)		(0.130)		(0.125)	
	Callrate_lag	0.671	***	0.682	***	0.665	***
		(0.028)		(0.039)		(0.037)	
Transition Probability	Constant	1.01	***	-0.077		0.065	
		(0.088)		(0.204)		(0.205)	
	Netmvmt	0.123	***			0.152	***
		(0.02)				(0.035)	
	Exres			0.103	***	0.089	***
				(0.017)		(0.017)	
Panic							
Conditional Mean	Constant	-0.284		-0.261		-0.498	
		(0.192)		(1.089)		(0.955)	
	Callrate_lag	0.541	***	0.671	**	0.737	***
		(0.102)		(0.306)		(0.271)	
Conditional Variance	Constant	-3.929	***	1.409	***	1.283	***
		(0.311)		(0.432)		(0.435)	
	Callrate_lag	1.393	***	0.282	***	0.303	***
		(0.081)		(0.064)		(0.066)	
Transition Probability	Constant	-0.767	***	-0.271		-0.544	***
		(0.192)		(0.364)		(0.184)	
	Netmvmt	-0.098	**			-0.023	
		(0.038)				(7.964)	
	exres			-0.039		-0.054	
				(0.039)		(18.758)	
Value of Objective Function =		-1024.1		-1046.5		-1034.4	

Note: Standard errors are in parentheses.
* Indicates significance at the 10% level.
** Indicates significance at the 5% level.
*** Indicates significance at the 1% level.

Excess reserves, *exres*, which are the amount of reserves in the money-center

banks minus the amount of reserves that the money-center banks were required to hold, also seem to have a significant effect on the probability of a panic occurring. Again higher levels of reserves protected against the onset of a panic, while depleted reserves increased the probability of a crisis occurring.

In the rightmost column of table 4 we also consider the possibility that net movements and excess reserves might be measuring the same thing. We found that when they were run together, both were significant. This result indicates that both flows from the money-center banks and the level of reserves that banks held, contributed to the probability of entering a panic period.

In table 5 we show the results for the inclusion of international variables. Specifically, we looked at the possible effects that changes in the Bank of England discount rate, changes in the U.S. dollar–British pound exchange rate, and the net outflow of gold had on the probability of transitioning into or out of a crisis. Column 2 has the results for the changes in the Bank of England discount rate, but these changes did not have a significant effect. Similarly, the changes in the dollar/pound exchange rate did not appear to have a triggering effect. Freidman and Schwartz (1963) and Tallman and Moen (1998) discuss the effect of gold flows on the money supply in this period, but the weekly outflows of gold (column 4) do not appear to have had an effect in triggering panics.[11]

---

[11] The result for the panic period, however, seems to indicate that inflows of gold are associated with increasing the probability of staying in a panic state. A caveat to this result is that weekly net gold flows were a highly unstable series, and the optimization routine had difficulties finding a stable result with this variable. In later versions of the paper we will continue refining the use of this variable.

Table 5:
International Variables

	Independent Variables	Change in BoE Discount Rate		Change in $/£ exchange rate		Net Gold Flow	
Normal							
Conditional Mean	Constant	0.004		0.046	**	-0.038	***
		(0.033)		(0.023)		(0.003)	
	Callrate_lag	0.017		-0.046	**	0.061	***
		(0.020)		(0.018)		(0.007)	
Conditional Variance	Constant	-4.785	***	-8.062	***	-3.890	***
		(0.139)		(0.204)		(0.002)	
	Callrate_lag	1.293	***	2.358	***	1.087	***
		(0.034)		(0.073)		(0.011)	
Transition Probability	Constant	1.706	***	0.992	***	3.003	***
		(0.096)		(0.102)		(0.000)	
	ch_BoE	0.532					
		(0.374)					
	ch_exch			1.145			
				(23.278)			
	Goldflow					0.000	
						(0.000)	
Panic							
Conditional Mean	Constant	4.061	***	0.598	***	4.840	***
		(0.109)		(0.104)		(0.003)	
	Callrate_lag	-0.896	***	-0.137	***	-0.392	***
		(0.011)		(0.029)		(0.018)	
Conditional Variance	Constant	2.161	***	-1.622	***	3.509	***
		(0.611)		(0.139)		(0.000)	
	Callrate_lag	-0.833	***	0.360	***	-1.676	***
		(0.143)		(0.023)		(0.000)	
Transition Probability	Constant	0.555	***	1.161	***	0.972	***
		(0.152)		(0.096)		(0.000)	
	ch_BoE	-0.646					
		(0.627)					
	ch_exch			0.060			
				(14.117)			
	Goldflow					0.001	***
						(0.000)	
Value of Objective Function =		-1435.73		-1010.98		-1529.36	

Note: Standard errors are in parentheses.
* Indicates significance at the 10% level.
** Indicates significance at the 5% level.
*** Indicates significance at the 1% level.

In table 6, we consider the variables most consistent with the insolvency-based banking panic. The changes in the value of the stock market (*pctchsv*), week to week, did not appear to affect the likelihood of a panic beginning. The coefficient does have a positive sign, the direction one would expect, but is not significant. This fact indicates that financial panics did not tend to spread from the stock market to the banking sector, and the declines in the stock market associated with banking panics might have spread from the banking sector to the stock market via substantial reductions in liquidity. Given the forward-looking nature of the stock market, we did not find evidence to support the assertion that stockholders were anticipating an economic downturn in advance of the start of a banking panic.

Commercial failures also did not appear to lead financial panics. When we used the change in commercial failures (*ch_fail*) to measure commercial health, an increase in failures had the expected sign but was not a significant predictor of an impending switch into a panic state.

Table 6:
Business Cycle Variables

	Independent Variables	Stock Market Change		Change in Commercial Failures	
Normal					
Conditional Mean	Constant	0.045	**	0.094	***
		(0.022)		(0.026)	
	Callrate_lag	-0.044	**	-0.048	***
		(0.018)		(0.014)	
Conditional Variance	Constant	-8.044	***	-4.224	***
		(0.200)		(0.144)	
	Callrate_lag	2.356	***	0.8	***
		(0.073)		(0.043)	
Transition Probability	Constant	1.009	***	1.526	***
		(0.103)		(0.088)	
	Pctchsv	-0.035			
		(0.048)			
	ch_commfail			-0.003	
				(0.002)	

Table 6 (cont.):
Time-Varying Transition Probabilities

Panic					
Conditional Mean	Constant	0.582	***	4.582	***
		(0.098)		(1.129)	
	Callrate_lag	-0.134	***	-0.461	***
		(0.027)		(0.172)	
Conditional Variance	Constant	-1.693	***	3.111	***
		(0.134)		(0.298)	
	Callrate_lag	0.366	***	0.072	**
		(0.023)		(0.031)	
Transition Probability	Constant	1.184	***	0.103	
		(0.101)		(0.185)	
	pctchsv	0.073			
		(0.048)			
	ch_commfail			-0.005	
				(0.005)	
Value of Objective Function =		-1040.8		-1074.2	

Note: Standard errors are in parentheses.
* Indicates significance at the 10% level.
** Indicates significance at the 5% level.
*** Indicates significance at the 1% level.

The variables that were most significant in explaining the triggers of panics were the net movement of funds from the money-center banks to the country banks, and the level of excess reserves. Those two variables were complementary, and each enhanced the effect of the other. As excess reserves fell and deposits flowed out of the reserve banks, the probability of entering a crisis increased. These findings suggest that panics were a function of the declines in deposits and reserves, and they lend support to the theories of Kemmerer (1910), Eichengreen (1984), Chari and Jagannathan (1988), and others who are mentioned above.

Also interesting to note were those variables that did not have an effect on the probability of entering a crisis: the stock market, business failures, changes in the Bank of England discount rate, and changes in the exchange rate. The lack of significance of the stock market variable is particularly interesting because it indicates that the transmission of these panics might have gone from the banking sector to the stock market. Also the stock market is forward looking, so any expectation of impending recession should have shown up there first. Taken together, the lack of significance of both the business failures variable and the stock market variable in affecting the chances of moving into a panic state would tend to suggest that movements into a financial panic were not based on an expectation of an economic downturn and lowered business profits, as Calomiris and Gorton (1991) suggest.

The international factors did not appear to play a strong role in triggering panics. Changes in the Bank of England discount rate and flows of gold out of the United States did not appear to have the strong effect on triggering these panics that Sprague (1910) and Tallman and Moen (1998) suggest.

Conclusion

First of all, the Markov Switching Model using the interest rate from the callable loan market does a very good job of picking out the periods of panic from the normal periods in the National Banking Era. The dates that the model finds are similar to the dates of banking panics found by other authors, but the model uses an objective mechanism derived from the data themselves. Our use of weekly data gives more precision to the dates for the onset and conclusion of panics and allows us to examine the possible triggers of panic periods more accurately.

In studying the onsets of these panic periods, we have found that the net movement of deposits away from the money-center banks and low levels of excess reserves greatly increased the probability of financial panics between 1890 and 1909. This finding lends support to the theories of the contemporaries of these banking panics, such as Kemmerer (1910), as well as to the more recent work by Miron (1986), Eichengreen (1984), and Chari and Jagannathan (1988).

Equally important in many ways are the variables that were not significantly related to the onset of panics, such as changes in stock market values. The lack of significance for stock market changes suggests that falls in the stock market did not set off banking panics; rather, if stocks fell while banks were more troubled, the causality may well have run in the other direction—through a loss of liquidity in the call market. Also, we did not find support for the cause of bank panics hypothesized by Calomiris and Gorton (1991) and others; the theory that bank panics stem from a general change in sentiment in the economy about the prospects of business profits. Stocks are a forward-looking measure of economic activity, and neither stocks nor the variable measuring business failures was a significant predictor of an impending banking panic.

Appendix

The state variable, S_t, takes on a value of one if a panic period occurs, and it equals zero if such an event does not occur. This variable identifies the state of the economy, and these states are assumed to be path dependent and to evolve according to a first-order Markov process. The likelihood of moving between states is measured by transition probabilities, and according to the first-order Markov structure, these probabilities depend only on the state the process is in at $t-1$. Information on states earlier than $t-1$ is not relevant to the transition probability; however, these probabilities may be influenced by a number of other factors in the model, where the transition probabilities are allowed to vary over time.

The model assumes random movement between states, and the transition probabilities define the likelihood of shifting between states. The transition probability $\Pr(S_t = 1 \mid S_{t-1} = 0, x_t)$ defines the likelihood of shifting into the panic state. The probability of staying in the same state is the same as 1 minus the probability of transitioning into a panic state, or $1 - \Pr(S_t = 1 \mid S_{t-1} = 0, x_t)$, where x_t represents variables that affect the probability of transition. Thus a decline in $\Pr(S_t = 0 \mid S_{t-1} = 0, x_t)$ increases the likelihood of shifting into a financial panic. It is possible to incorporate transition probabilities that change over time and may be influenced by other factors. By identifying the factors that influence the transition probability $\Pr(S_t = 0 \mid S_{t-1} = 0, x_t)$, we can determine the causes or triggers of these financial panics. For example, one might establish that $\Pr(S_t = 0 \mid S_{t-1} = 0, x_t)$ is positively related to some measures of macroeconomic activity. In this case, the significance of these variables would confirm that the likelihood of a panic increased as the macroeconomy was moving into a recession.

One of the objectives of this paper is to determine the causes of historical financial crises by identifying variables that influence the transition probability $\Pr(S_t = 0 \mid S_{t-1} = 0, x_t)$. Moreover, since $\Pr(S_t = 0 \mid S_{t-1} = 1, x_t) = 1 - \Pr(S_t = 1 \mid S_{t-1} = 1, x_t)$ determines the likelihood of shifting out of a crisis, we also examine factors contributing to ending a crisis. We will perform this part of the analysis by identifying variables that influence the transition probability $\Pr(S_t = 1 \mid S_{t-1} = 1, x_t)$. Of course, since $\Pr(S_t = 1 \mid S_{t-1} = 1, x_t)$ defines the likelihood of remaining in a panic from one period to the next, parameterizing this probability also provides an opportunity to identify factors that might have prolonged a crisis.

The observed variable is change in the call market interest rate, that is, $\Delta r_t \equiv r_t - r_{t-1}$. Using S_t, an observation from a given state can be expressed as

$$\Delta r_t \equiv \mu[\theta_\mu(S_t), \Phi_{t-1}] + \sqrt{h[\theta_h(S_t), \Phi_{t-1}]}\, z_t \qquad (A.1)$$

where θ_μ and θ_h are vectors of unknown parameters, Φ_{t-1} is the agent's information set at time $t-1$, and z_t is again an independent and identically distributed random variable with mean zero and unit variance.

For notational convenience, equation (A.1) is rewritten as

$$\Delta r_t \equiv \mu_{it} + \sqrt{h_{it}}\, z_t \qquad (A.2)$$

for $S_t = i$. Here, for a given state S_t, the terms μ_{it} and h_{it} define the conditional mean and conditional variance, respectively.

Interest rates tend to be mean reverting. In order to have the flexibility to capture mean reversion if it should be the case in our specification, our model allows the change in the short rate to depend linearly on the level of last period's short rate. The functional form of the conditional mean is specified by

$$\mu_{it} = a_{0i} + a_{1i} r_{t-1}. \qquad (A.3)$$

Another common trait of interest rates is to be leptokurtic. In order to control for the possibility of conditional variance, we specified the variance process as

$$h_{it} = \exp(b_{0i} + b_{1i}r_{t-1}).\tag{A.4}$$

Interest rates appear to be higher and more volatile during panic periods, and we model these differences in the level and volatility of interest rates by specifying a unique data-generating process for each regime. In equation (A.1), the variable S_t identifies the regime, and the conditional mean and conditional variance are then defined as functions of this state variable. Assuming normality for each regime, the conditional distribution of Δr_t is the mixture of $N(\mu_{0t}, h_{0t})$ for regime 0 and $N(\mu_{1t}, h_{1t})$ for regime 1. More formally, the conditional distribution of Δr_t is written as

$$\Delta r_t \mid \Phi_{t-1} \sim \begin{cases} N(\mu_{0t}, h_{ot}) & \text{with probability } p_{0t} \\ N(\mu_{1t}, h_{1t}) & \text{with probability } p_{1t} \end{cases}\tag{A.5}$$

where $p_{0t} = \Pr(S_t = 0 \mid \Phi_{t-1})$ is the ex ante probability of regime 0 and $p_{1t} = 1 - \Pr(S_t = 0 \mid \Phi_{t-1})$ is the ex ante probability of regime 1.

The model characterizes interest rates as realizations from either a panic or a non-panic state. However, the states are not perfectly observable, and the assumption of a mixed distribution accounts for the uncertainty surrounding the unobserved states. The density function for a given interest rate regime can be written as

$$f(\Delta r_t \mid S_t) \equiv i, \Phi_{t-1} \equiv \frac{1}{\sqrt{2\pi h_{it}}} \exp\{\frac{-(\Delta r_t - \mu_{it})^2}{2h_{it}}\}.\tag{A.6}$$

The joint density-distribution function of Δr_t and S_t can be expressed as

$$p(\Delta r_t, S_t \equiv i \mid \Phi_{t-1}) \equiv p_{it} \frac{1}{\sqrt{2\pi h_{it}}} \exp\{\frac{-(\Delta r_t - \mu_{it})^2}{2h_{it}}\}.\tag{A.7}$$

Using this expression, we can write the density function for the mixed distribution as

33

$$f(\Delta r_t \mid \Phi_{t-1}) \equiv p_{0t} \frac{1}{\sqrt{2\pi h_{0t}}} \exp\{\frac{-(\Delta r_t - \mu_{0t})^2}{2h_{0t}}\} + p_{1t} \frac{1}{\sqrt{2\pi h_{1t}}} \exp\{\frac{-(\Delta r_t - \mu_{1t})^2}{2h_{1t}}\}. \quad (A.8)$$

For a given state, the density function in equation (A.6) represents a measure of the probability of observing a sample value. The density function in equation (A.8) is the weighted average of the different state density-functions, where the weights are the probabilities of the states. By weighting the state density functions in this way, the mixed distribution allows for the possibility that an observation could be associated with either state. Such a specification is appropriate, given the uncertainty surrounding the states. Since the states are not perfectly observable, one could never know with certainty that an observation was associated with a particular state. For example, although a very high interest rate would most likely be associated with the volatile interest-rate state, such a realization could always represent a tail event from the other state.

As the states are unobservable, one needs to refer to a state by a probability measure. The ex ante probabilities from equation (A.5) correspond to the state probabilities. These probabilities are determined on the basis of the information that is available before the realization of Δr_t. An ex post probability improves on this inference by using information about the time t observation of the dependent variable. By Bayes' Rule, equations (A.7) and (A.8) can be used to determine the ex post probability as

$$\begin{aligned} \Pr(S_t \equiv k \mid \Phi_t) &\equiv \Pr(S_t \equiv k \mid \Phi_{t-1}, \Delta r_t) \\ &\equiv \frac{p(\Delta r_t, S_t = k \mid \Phi_{t-1})}{f(\Delta r_t \mid \Phi_{t-1})} \end{aligned} \quad (A.9)$$

The ex ante probabilities can be interpreted as the likelihood that the time t observation of the dependent variable is associated with a given interest-rate distribution. These probabilities depend in part on the regime in place in the prior period. The ex ante probability would equal the transition probability if the prior state were known with certainty. For example, $\Pr(S_t = 0 \mid \Phi_{t-1}) = \Pr(S_t = 0 \mid S_{t-1} = 0, x_t)$ if one knew with certainty that the prior period was a time of relatively stable interest rates. In this case, this state probability would be determined by the likelihood of remaining in $S_t = 0$ from one period to the next, $\Pr(S_t = 0 \mid S_{t-1} = 0, x_t)$.

Unfortunately, the state cannot be observed with certainty. Consequently, one must account for the possibility that the process could have been in either state in the prior period. To account for this uncertainty, one determines the ex ante probability by weighting the transition probabilities by probability measures of the prior state. An expression for the ex ante probability of a non-crisis state can be written as

$$\Pr(S_t = 0 \mid \Phi_{t-1}) = \sum_{i=0}^{1} \Pr(S_{t-1} = i \mid \Phi_{t-1}) \Pr(S_t = 0 \mid S_{t-1} = i, x_t). \qquad (A.10)$$

Equation (A.10) defines the ex ante probability as the sum of two terms, where each term is the product of an ex post probability and a transition probability. Similarly, an expression for the ex ante probability of a crisis state can be written as

$$\Pr(S_t = 1 \mid \Phi_{t-1}) = \sum_{i=0}^{1} \Pr(S_{t-1} = i \mid \Phi_{t-1}) \Pr(S_t = 1 \mid S_{t-1} = i, x_t). \qquad (A.11)$$

The model specifies two states, where each state is characterized by a unique interest-rate distribution. However, since the states cannot be observed with certainty, the sample values are viewed as realizations from a mixture of the two interest-rate distributions. Equations (A.10) and (A.11) define the ex ante probabilities as weighted averages of the transition probabilities. After substituting the expressions for the ex ante probabilities into the density function in equation (A.8), one observes that the parameters of the mixed distribution necessarily include the parameters of the transition probabilities. Thus, estimates for these (and all other) parameters can be obtained by the use of observations from the mixed distribution. In other words, inferences about the unknown parameters use actual observations of short-term interest rates.

However, this estimation requires additional specification of the transition probabilities. Using an algorithm developed by Hamilton (1989), we obtain parameter estimates by means of maximum-likelihood estimation. The transition probabilities are further clarified as

$$
\begin{aligned}
\Pr(S_t = 0 \mid S_{t-1} = 0, x_t) &= p(x_t; \beta_p) \\
\Pr(S_t = 1 \mid S_{t-1} = 0, x_t) &= 1 - p(x_t; \beta_p) \\
\Pr(S_t = 1 \mid S_{t-1} = 1, x_t) &= q(x_t; \beta_q) \\
\Pr(S_t = 0 \mid S_{t-1} = 1, x_t) &= 1 - q(x_t; \beta_q)
\end{aligned}
\tag{A.12}
$$

where p and q are specified as cumulative normal distribution functions. Maximum-likelihood estimation involves choosing parameters that maximize the value of a likelihood function. In equation (A.12), the functional form of p and q maps the variables x_t into the open interval $(0,1)$ and thereby guarantees a well-defined likelihood function.

References

Ang, Andrew, and Geert Bekaert. 2002. Regime Switches in Interest Rates. *Journal of Business and Economic Statistics* 20(2):163–82.

Bhattacharya, Sudipto, and Douglas M. Gale. 1987. Preference Shocks, Liquidity, and Central Bank Policy. In *New Approaches to Monetary Economics*, edited by William A. Barnett and Kenneth J. Singleton, 69–88. New York: Cambridge University Press

Bollerslev, Tim. 1986. Generalized Autoregressive Conditional Heteroskedasticity. *Journal of Econometrics* 31:307–27.

Bordo, Michael D., Angela Redish, and Hugh Rockoff. 1996. A Comparison of the Stability and Efficiency of the Canadian and American Banking Systems 1870–1925. NBER Historical Paper no. 67, November.

Calomiris, Charles W., and Gary Gorton. 1991. The Origins of Banking Panics: Models, Facts and Bank Regulation. In *Financial Markets and Financial Crises*, edited by R. G. Hubbard, 109–73. Chicago: University of Chicago Press.

Cannon, James Graham. 1910. *Clearing Houses*. National Monetary Commission, 61st Cong., 2nd sess. Senate Document 491. Washington, DC: Government Printing Office.

Canova, Fabio. 1994. Were Financial Crises Predictable? *Journal of Money, Credit, and Banking* 26:102–24.

Champ, Bruce, Bruce D. Smith, and Stephen D. Williamson. 1996. Currency Elasticity and Banking Panics: Theory and Evidence. *Canadian Journal of Economics* 29(4):828–64.

Chari, V. V. 1989. Banking Without Deposit Insurance or Bank Panics: Lessons from a Model of the U.S. National Banking System. Federal Reserve Bank of Minneapolis *Quarterly Review* 13(3):3–19.

Chari, V. V. and Ravi Jagannathan. 1988. Banking Panics, Information, and Rational Expectations Equilibrium. *Journal of Finance* 43:749–61.

Dewald, William G. 1972. The National Monetary Commission: A Look Back. *Journal of Money, Credit, and Banking* 4(4):930–56.

Diamond, Douglas W., and Philip Dybvig. 1983. Bank Runs, Deposit Insurance, and Liquidity. *Journal of Political Economy* 91:401–19.

Donaldson, R. Glenn. 1992. Sources of Panics. *Journal of Monetary Economics* 30:277–305.

Eichengreen, Barry. 1984. Currency and Credit in the Gilded Age. In *Technique, Spirit and Form in Making Modern Economics*, edited by Gary Saxonhouse and Gavin Wright, 87–114. Westport, CT: JAI Press.

Engle, Robert F. 1982. Autoregressive Conditional Heteroskedasticity with Estimates of U.K. Inflation. *Econometrica* 50:987–1008.

Friedman, Milton, and Anna J. Schwartz. 1963. *A Monetary History of the United States, 1867–1960*. Princeton: Princeton University Press.

Garcia, Rene. 1998. Asymptotic Null Distribution of the Likelihood Ratio Test in Markov Switching Models. *International Economic Review* 39(3):763–88.

Gorton, Gary. 1988. Banking Panics and Business Cycles. *Oxford Economic Journal* 40:751–81.

Gray, Steven F. 1996. Modeling the Conditional Distribution of Interest Rates as a Regime Switching Process. *Journal of Financial Economics* 42:27–62.

Hamilton, James D. 1989. A New Approach to the Economic Analysis of Nonstationary Time Series and the Business Cycle. *Econometrica* 57(2):357–84.

Jevons, W. Stanley. 1884. *Investigation in Currency and Finance.* London: Macmillan.

Kemmerer, E. W. 1910. *Seasonal Variations in the Relative Demand for Money and Capital in the United States: A Statistical Study*. National Monetary Commission, 61st Cong., 2nd sess. Senate Document 588. Washington, DC: Government Printing Office.

Kindleberger, Charles P. 1978. *Manias, Panics, and Crashes: A History of Financial Crises*. New York: John Wiley & Sons, Inc.

Miron, Jeffrey A. 1986. Financial Panics, the Seasonality of the Nominal Interest Rate, and the Founding of the Fed. *American Economic Review* 76:125–40.

Moen, Jon R., and Ellis W. Tallman. 2003. The Call Loan Market in the U.S. Financial System Prior to the Federal Reserve System. Working Paper Series, no. 2003-43. Federal Reserve Bank of Atlanta.

Myers, Margaret G. 1931. *The New York Money Market,* vol. 1, *Origins and Development*. New York: Columbia University Press.

Sprague, O. M. W. 1910. *History of Crises under the National Banking System*. National Monetary Commission, 61st Cong., 2nd sess. Senate Document 538. Washington, DC: Government Printing Office.

Tallman, Ellis, and Jon Moen. 1998. Gold Shocks, Liquidity, and the United States Economy during the National Banking Era. *Explorations in Economic History* 35:381–404.

Williamson, Stephen D. 1989. Bank Failures, Financial Restriction, and Aggregate Fluctuations: Canada and the United States, 1870–1913. Federal Reserve Bank of Minneapolis *Quarterly Review* 13(3):20–40.

Figure 1
Call Market Interest Rate

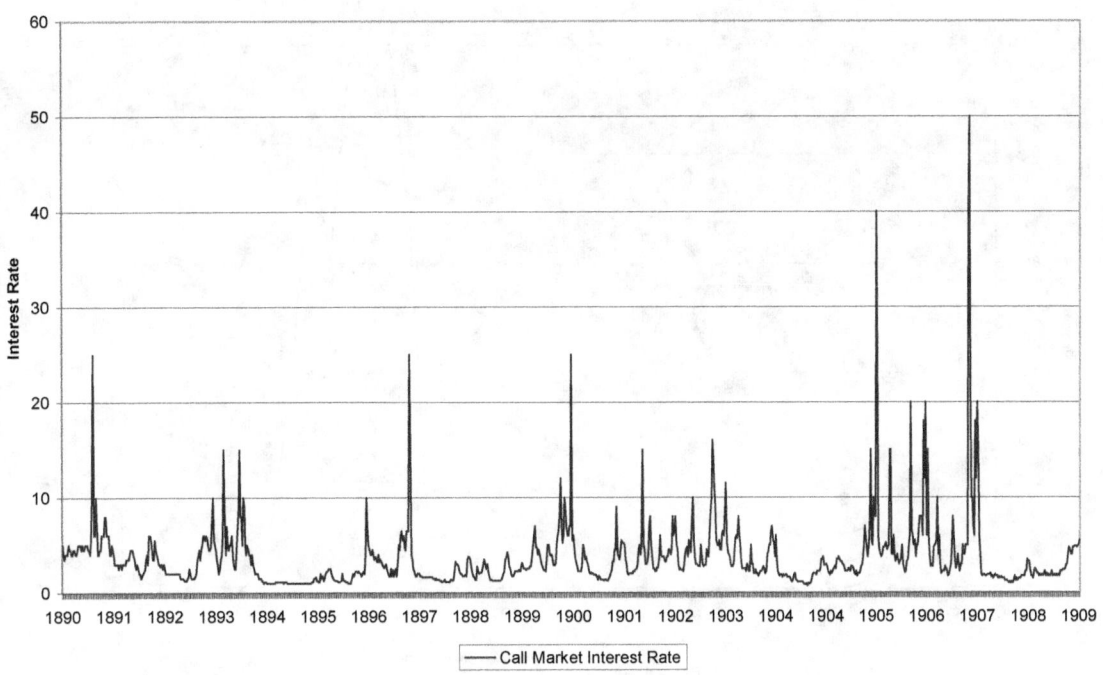

Figure 2
Change in Call Market Interest Rate

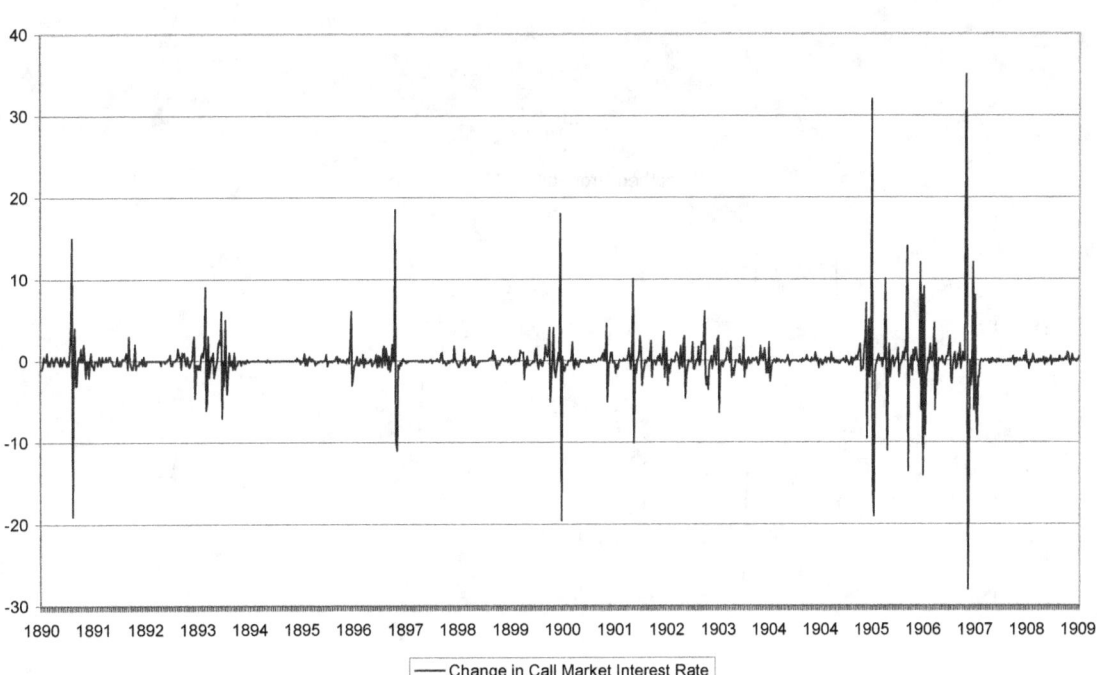

Figure 3
1890
Smoothed Probability of Panic State

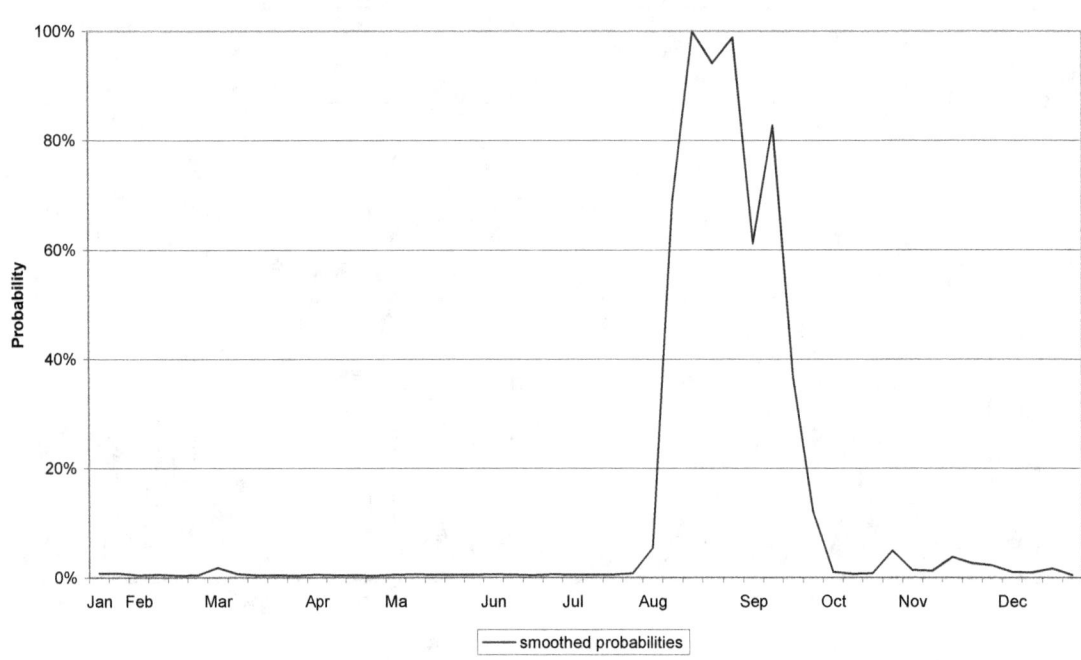

Figure 4
1893
Smoothed Probability of Panic State

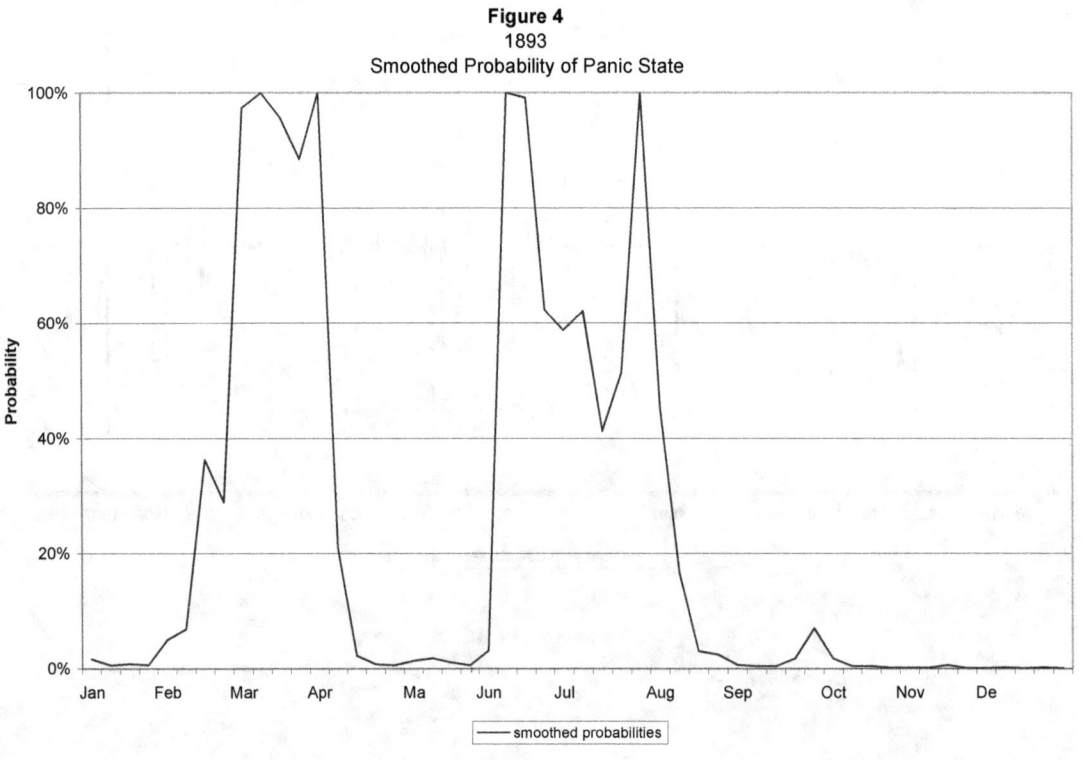

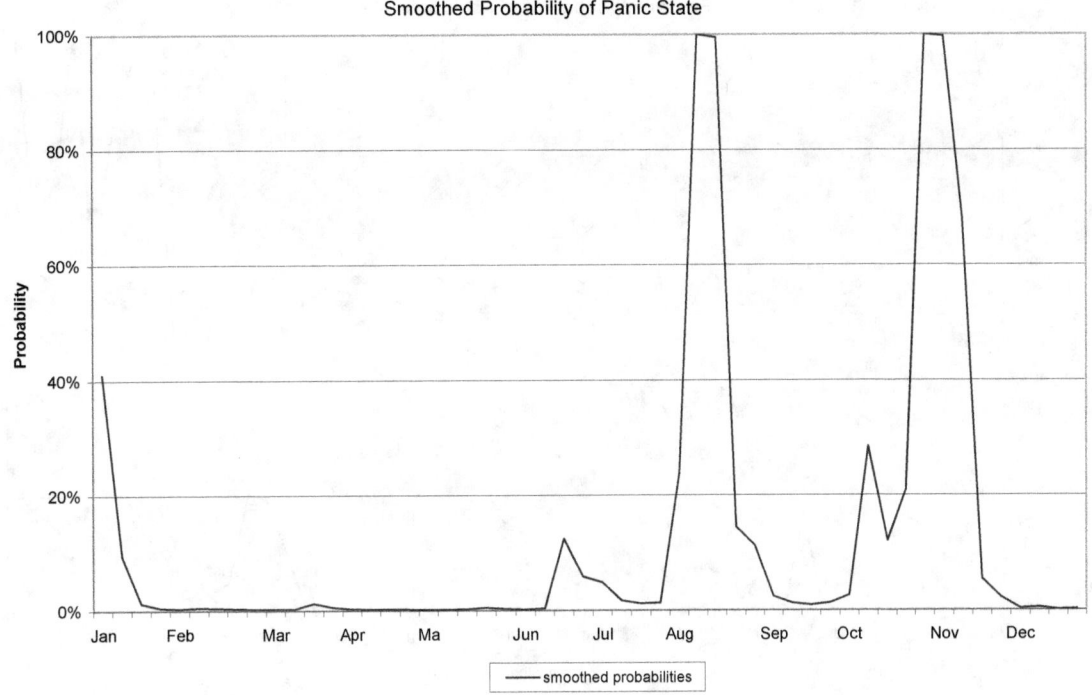

Figure 5
1896
Smoothed Probability of Panic State

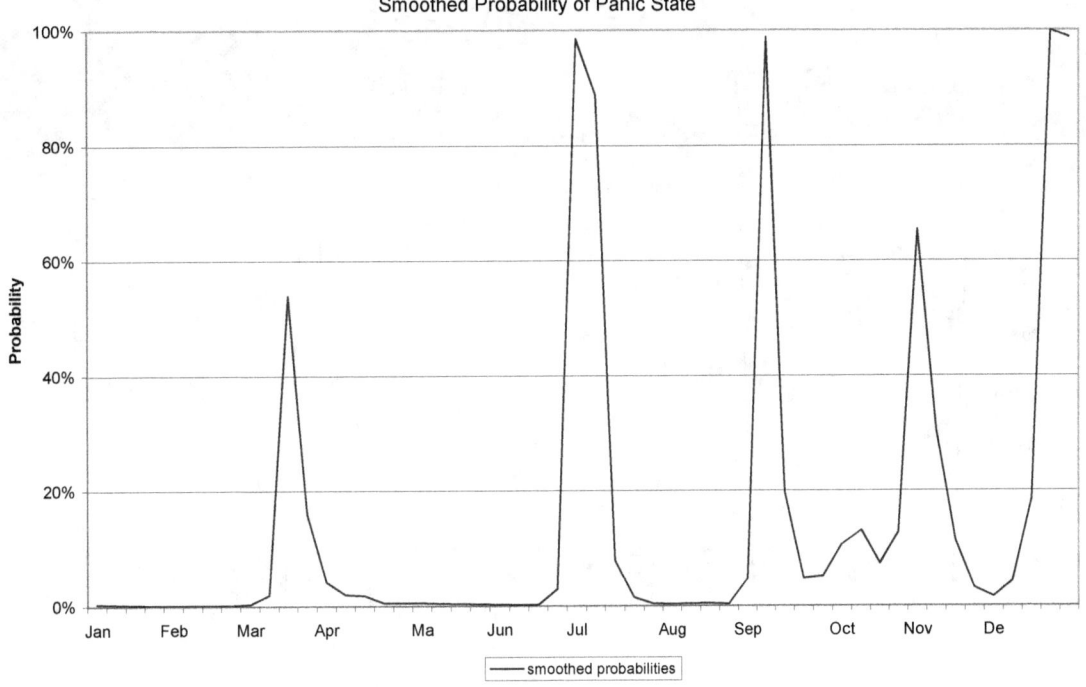

Figure 6
1899
Smoothed Probability of Panic State

41

Figure 7
1905
Smoothed Probability of Panic State

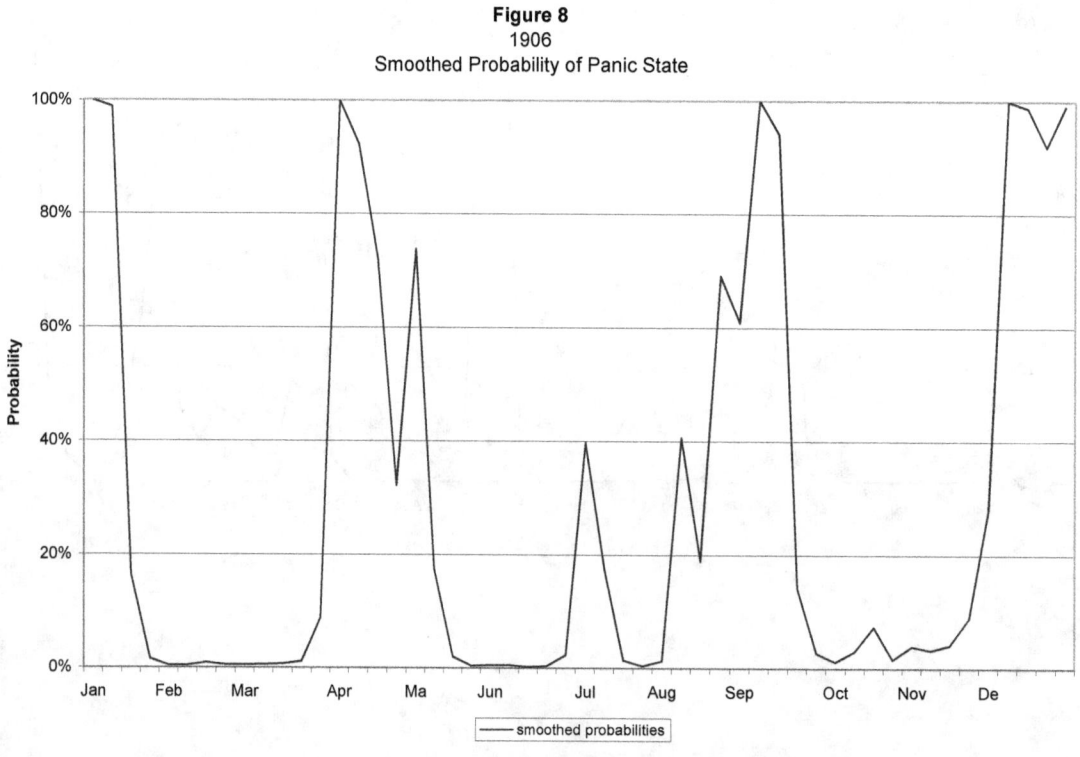

Figure 8
1906
Smoothed Probability of Panic State

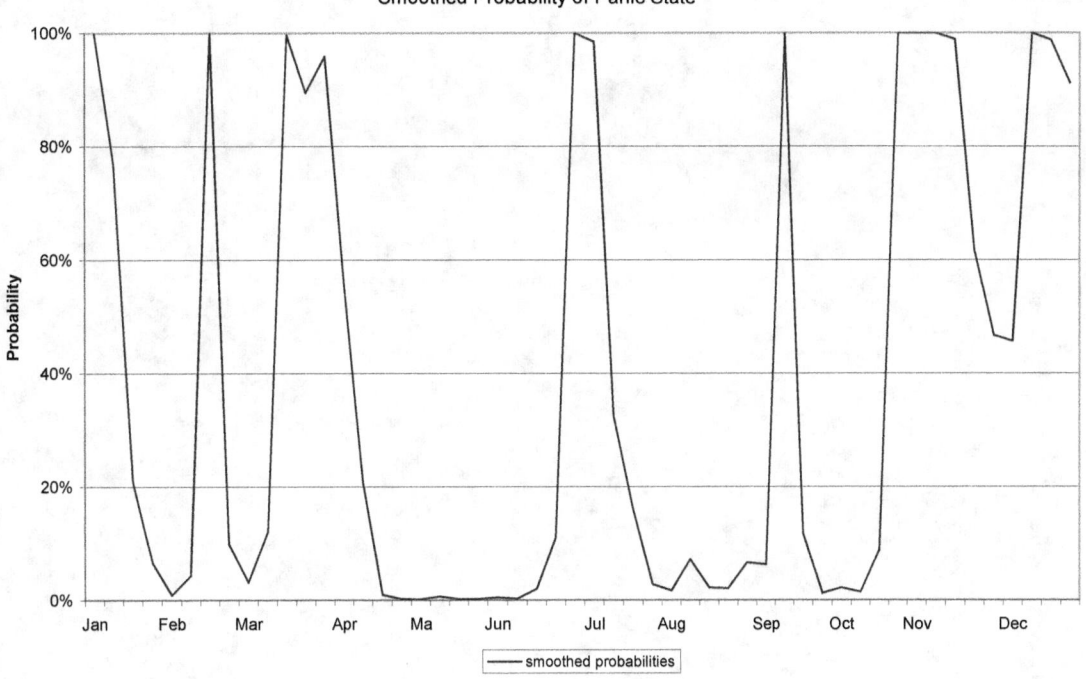

Figure 9
1907
Smoothed Probability of Panic State